Exhale
Before Bed

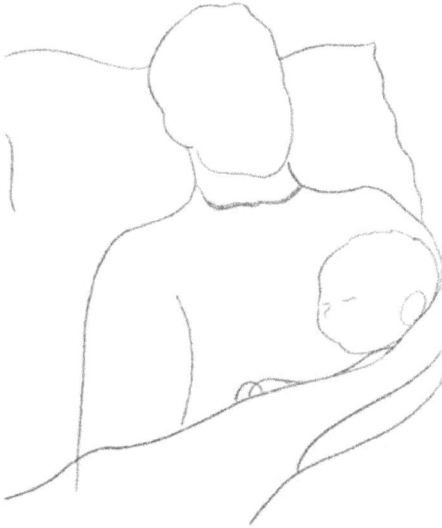

Deana Steyn

Exhale
Before Bed

Daily Reflections Before Bed

By Deana Steyn

Published By
Eagles Word Christian Publisher
New York

Dedicated to

Jesus, my everything.

My husband, Shaun; my best friend.

My children, Daniel, Bevan and Jordan-Lee
whom I love more than life.

Author's Note

Reflecting at the end of each day allows us to observe, pause and extract meaning from our experiences. This aids in our peace.

Our last few minutes before we go to sleep make a difference to our sleep quality, our dreams and our consciousness. Our spirit doesn't sleep.

Some say the first thing in the morning is what sets the tone for the day. I believe that the last thing that you fill your mind with before going to sleep has a huge impact on how the following day will proceed.

As you settle into bed each night, before you turn off your lamp, take time for yourself to pause and contemplate by reading one short entry.

I hope that you enjoy exhaling before you fall asleep through these words!!

These reflections are short and explore various themes of Self, Circle, Living, Ponder, Nature and Source. They can be read in any order you choose. At the end of the day, we are tired so the writing style is simple and straightforward. Most entries are inspired by personal experience.

Scriptures are referenced at the end of the book.

"God can provide for His devoted lovers even while they sleep"
Psalm 127:2

Contents

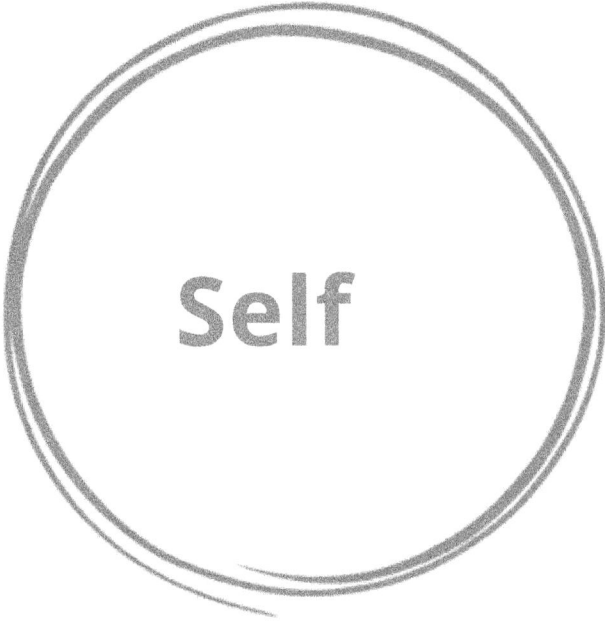

Self

I Need More

This entry is inspired by a very brave woman that I know. She built up the courage to say the above phrase one morning: "I need more". How empowering these three words are. Verbalising something that you need (which is different from what you want) is from the heart. Being daring enough to communicate that you are not happy with the way things are, is brave.

These three words inspired me. So simple and yet so profoundly truthful. What do I need more of? More time? More space? More family time? More understanding? More money? How long have I been going through my days on auto pilot, doing, talking, watching, writing, reading, working, eating, sleeping without giving thought to what I need in my life?

At the time of writing this, I needed more space to work. My husband works from home and my daughter was also working from home at this time. Our home isn't large and the communal area is open where we eat and sit. I asked my family to note that if my bedroom door is closed, that I am not wanting to be disturbed, that I was having time alone.

It worked! Verbalising what I needed led to having the space I needed without changing our circumstances.

Reflect:

What do you need? Do you communicate what you need, or do you expect others to know what you need? Could you tell someone this week about something that you need?

Your Voice

Did you ever stop to think that most of our lives we listen to other people? When we are babies, we listen to the voice of our parents telling us what to do and what not to do. This continues throughout childhood. We then attend school and listen to what the teachers tell us to do. Then when we leave school, some of us continue to listen to the voice of others.

Do you remember a time when you used your own voice to ask for something or to verbalize an opinion? Didn't you feel alive? Didn't you feel empowered? Is your voice still there?

It's time to hear your own voice. It is that knowing deep down inside of you where you and God know what you want to do. Being who you truly are and being authentic is worth more than pleasing others around you. Ultimately, parents want their child to be happy. Live your original life.

Reflect:

Do you feel like others tell you what to do?
When last did you use your own voice?

Could you ask God for courage to stand up to those
who expect you to be who you are not?

You are worth it.

"Should"

Do you find yourself using the word "should" in conversation with others or inside your own head? "I *should* be doing this because I am a mom, I *should* be earning at least this.., I *should* weigh less/more, I *should* have my life in order by now, I *should* know how to do certain things by now." and the list goes on.

Who are these people who cause us to use the word "should"? Do you know them? Who says you should make your children's lunches for school if you are a mother of small children? Who says we should earn a certain amount of money? Who is putting these thoughts into our heads?

The Bible says in Micah 6:8 that God has made it plain how to live, what to do, and that it's quite simple:
Do what is fair and just to your neighbour, be compassionate and loyal in your love, and don't take yourself too
seriously – take God seriously.

If we look at the scripture above, I am not sure if we need to have all these "shoulds" in our lives. If we act fairly with others, love them, and walk humbly with our God, we are doing what we "should" be doing. The other rules we give ourselves are from our culture, our social groups, social media, and expectations of others.

Reflect:

The next time someone tells you what you should be doing, or you hear someone telling you what they should be doing, could you challenge it?

3

Does Appearance Matter?

One day when I was at church, a man stood up and started talking about what Jesus looked like. He said that many of us find it hard to picture Jesus. Nothing much is said about his appearance in the Bible. He said that if we want to know what Jesus is like, we can look at his characteristics. He was patient, humble, uncompromising, kind, strong, loyal and served those around him. It got me thinking.

If the Son of God's appearance isn't mentioned in the Bible – I mean one of the Apostles could have mentioned the length of His hair or the colour of His eyes – then perhaps appearance is not as important as we make it out to be.

I love spending time with friends who make me feel happy, who make me feel lighter after being in their company. I really don't care what they look like at all. It's how I feel in their presence and how I feel after being with them that matters. Why then do we place such importance on how we look? Yes, we need to shower and be presentable but let's not get obsessed. Let's rather work on who we are; let's see how beautiful we are on the inside! It's what counts, after all.

Reflect:

As you fall asleep tonight, realise that you are good enough.
It's your heart that is the most attractive thing about you.

Plans or Dreams?

Do we want our dreams to become reality or do we want them to remain as dreams?

When I say, "I dream of going to India with my daughter" I do actually mean that I want to go before I die. But what about the "how"? What do I have in place or in motion that will move that dream into a reality? Am I planning to make it happen?

I find that I have many dreams. I dream of being healthy and being the best version of myself, but when I sit and eat a pizza and drink a bottle of wine, it's not going to get me there. I fall short on the "how". What do I need to do? Step by step, what do I need to change?

Generally, we all want similar things. What makes some people attain their dreams and others not? Perhaps it's in the execution, in the methods used. I like to browse through online accommodation sites and daydream about what we will do and where we will go. Yet, I do not get quotes for visas, air tickets, accommodation and tours or put a savings plan in place.

Reflect:

What are some of your dreams? What would it take to make them happen?

What are the methods you need to follow? What one step could you take to make this dream into a closer reality?

Treasure Hunt

When last did you feel really okay? Content, happy, accepted? Was it yesterday or five years ago? When did you last feel happy, healthy, energetic? Like you belonged somewhere, that you are enough, that you are worthy?

Come on a treasure hunt with me and look for moments in your day when you felt okay. Bring an awareness to how you felt today. Notice how you felt when you were with certain people or doing certain things.

Chances are that if we are more aware of moments when we feel okay, we can do more of them and empower ourselves. We will do the opposite to the people and activities that make us feel unwanted and not okay. Granted, some situations and people cannot be avoided but becoming aware of how we feel can bring a consciousness, a realization and a reason for why we feel the way we do.

Reflect:

When do you feel like you don't fit in? When do you feel like you don't belong? Who makes you feel like this and where are you when it happens?

Do you believe you are worthy of feeling okay?

Self-care or Selfishness

I don't know about you, but I want to take care of myself. I live in a body and without it I cannot do much. If we don't take care of our bodies, no matter how much we want to do something or go somewhere, we may not be able to do so.

We can love God and serve Him and feed the poor and go to the most dire places in the name of God, but if we wear ourselves out we are no good to anyone.

So how do we balance it? How do we nuture our minds, souls, spirits and bodies and also be available to what God is calling us to? If the pendulum swings too far to either side, we have missed it.

Perhaps we are supposed to be where God has placed us. Perhaps as we notice others in our immediate surroundings and reach out, it is less tiresome than crossing a continent. If God speaks, we listen; and if He tells us to cross a continent He will sustain us and give us stamina and strength. But trying to save the world in your own strength would leave families destroyed and people burnt out.

Reflect:

Do you feel guilty about taking time for yourself? Do you feel bad about going for a body massage or a long walk?

Is there a prize for the busiest and most exhausted?

Be Still

Our minds don't stop. Thoughts constantly rush through our heads with lists of things to do, people to call and commitments to keep. When does it stop?

Being aware of our thoughts means we have more chance of controlling them. Our thoughts have substance over which we can have influence. If we consciously tell our thoughts to fly away, and we start to notice the sights and sounds around us, we will be amazed at the difference. Space is created to just be, to breathe, to be still. Amazing things start to happen when we allow this space in our lives.

The other day I took a walk down the road where we live. It is a relatively quiet road, and being in Africa, there are monkeys, mongeese and even duiker (small buck). I chose to leave my cell phone behind and started to notice the sights and sounds around me. The wind in the trees, the blue sky, the puffy clouds and the smell of fresh rain filled my senses. My thoughts drifted and I let them go. My mind was spacious. I walked on and stopped to watch two duiker rubbing their noses together. I had never seen that before. I shared the tenderness of this brief encounter with them.

Reflect:

Are you faced with a problem that seems insolvable? Are you in a situation where it seems there is no way out?

Can you acknowledge that some quiet space with your Heavenly Father might help?

Trajectory

One movie that really impacted me was "Rocket Man" which is based on the music and life of British musician, Elton John. Even if you have heard the song before, go ahead and listen to *Rocket Man*, turn up the volume and listen to the words.

Have you ever thought about the fact that God knows the path of your life? He is never going to leave you.

A friend of mine once sent me the word "trajectory". A trajectory is a course or path that is followed by an object under the action of a force. We are all on a course in life that sometimes meanders, sometimes there are highs and lows, but there is a path none the less.

God knows where we are going, we have done all the pilot work and now all we have to do is climb on the rocket and He knows where it is going to land.

Enjoy the ride and the views along the way. We can work together with a loving and accepting Father. He accepts all of our mistakes and faults and all that we intend to do and don't do. He is there. Our trajectory, our flight path, our route, is going to be worth the ride.

Reflect:

Do you believe that God has good plans for you?

Could you "climb" onto your rocket in your mind and trust Him?

Whatever You Believe, You're Right

It really got me thinking that if I believe I will not finish this book, I am right. If I believe I will aways suffer from migraines, I am right. If I believe I will get to spend Christmas with all three grown up children one day soon, I am right.

What are the sabotaging thoughts that come into your mind? How can you make small changes to believe that good things can and will happen? Whatever you believe you are right. You have the power inside you to affect your future. The Bible tells us in Proverbs 23:7 that whatever we believe in our heart so we are.

Reflect:

Could you give yourself permission to believe the best for tomorrow?

Could you decide not to take yourself and others so seriously?

And whatever you believe about tomorrow and tonight, you are right.

Saying Yes Means Saying No

A special friend of mine said this to me and I found it quite profound. When I say no to having too much wine at night, I am saying yes to waking up with a clear head and an early morning. When I say no to buying something online that I don't need, I am saying yes to saving and being wiser with my money.

Whatever we say yes to means that we are saying no to something else. Instead of focusing on what we should not do, perhaps if we focus on saying yes to something we should do, it will work out that we say no to the destructive patterns we are always trying to stop.

It's like we are flipping it over. I tend to focus on not doing something and trying so hard not to do it, that I end up doing just the thing that I don't want to do. The Bible mentions that Paul feels this way too sometimes (Romans 7:19).
I am going to choose to say yes to peace and then by default no to anxiety.

Reflect:

What are you going to choose to say yes to?

By the choice made above, what will you be saying no to?

Want to Escape?

At the time of writing this, I have been to Bali, Indonesia, once. I hope that by the time that this book is published, I will have been again. It is a place that makes my soul come alive. The problem is that in the past I have wanted to go to Bali to escape my life in South Africa - to escape the reality of everyday life where I live.

I have realised that getting away is a good thing to do, and travel is a luxury that can be enjoyed alone or with family. But needing to escape my life, and fantasizing about it, became a concern to me.

I guess it's all about the intention of our trip. Do we want to numb our pain and run away? When we run away to a distant place, *we* are still there. We cannot escape ourselves - and then there's the issue of returning home again.

Instead of running, we could perhaps seek out a quiet place, perhaps somewhere in nature. Here we can talk to our God who is our Creator and Healer, who knows us better than anyone, who loves us unconditionally, who never leaves us, and who never turns us away. Let Him know your inner world and feel His comfort and support while your body stays in one place. Allow the pain to pass through and face the truths from which you try to run away .

Reflect:

What are some of the things that you feel you want to escape from?

Past

The past is over. We all have things we regret or feel guilty about, it is a natural part of life's journey. Remember that every moment that got us to where we are today, is part of what made us who we are.

In the melody of our life's journey, we dance to its tune and blossom into the people we are today. It's okay to be you. You are enough.

Leave your past behind, don't take it into this next chapter of your life, you will have enough challenges to face without bringing up old regrets. It's over, it's gone. Love is worth more than visiting areas of your life that are long gone.

If this resonates with you, then it's only fair that the same applies to your partner. Don't bring up the past. Past girlfriends or boyfriends, past relationships don't have a place in your future. You have chosen each other. Just let it be.

There may be a time that you both share some past experiences as a way of a deeper connection and that is how this should be shared - voluntarily and initiated by the one sharing, not out of interrogation or accusation of the one asking. Listen when this happens, don't be hasty to speak and never judge. The person you are in love with chose you despite your past so offer him/her the same.

Reflect:

Could you accept that you are not the only one who has made mistakes? Let them go.

Schedule Something Pleasant

I was going through a tough time in my early 50's and was doing some research on natural ways to fight depression. "Schedule something pleasant" came up as one of seven things to do in the week, that was offered by the particular website.

We have responsibilities, family duties and chores to do. Could we schedule something pleasant in our diary even if it's once a week?

It may be meeting up with a friend, going for a pottery lesson, playing golf, going for a surf or sitting in your pjs with a good book.

The point is if we don't schedule it, it doesn't seem to happen.

Reflect:

When last did you schedule something pleasant?

Could you jouralize an enjoyable experience?

Time Out

There is something about airports that makes me feel like I belong to a group of people: the travellers. Total strangers, yet standing in the queue to board the plane, it feels like we share something in common. Have you ever noticed that calories don't matter to travellers either? They grab a toasted sandwich/chocolate/muffin and coffee once through the boarding gates with no regard for rules of any eating plan. They have crossed over to another world and have left home and reality with its rules behind them.

Years ago I was on a flight with my 18-year-old son. As I watched him sleeping next to me, head phones on, I stared at his face and wondered how time had passed so quickly. His world, so different from mine, his challenges and pressures foreign to me and yet for this weekend, something connected us - we were both travellers. No nagging about tidying his room or doing homework. Just two adults eating takeaways and chatting about things that involve no lists/requirements or commitments.

I was contemplating why it took becoming a traveller for me to notice this. It took me back to my mind and what dwells there. At home our minds seem to think the same routine things, yet when we leave our routine, it creates space in our minds, for new experiences and for change.

Reflect:

This week become conscious of your conversations with those you love.

Like Yourself?

During a therapy session, I was asked the question, "Do you like yourself?" It caught me off guard.

I knew that God loved me, that my husband and children loved me and of course that my mother loved me. But how about what I felt towards myself? Forget about love – did I even like myself?

The answer at the time the question was posed was, "No". No, I did not like myself. I had a lot of regrets about how I handled things in the past. I didn't like how I looked or how I acted. I wasn't a bad person, I just lacked confidence and acted weirdly when I felt insecure and I didn't like myself at these times.

I am not going to write a lengthy discussion about what I didn't like about myself. It was just a question that made me wish my time in the therapist's room was over. I wanted to bolt. Things got uncomfortable.

Reflect:

Do you like yourself?

Do you like who you have become?

Do you like how you treat others?

Life is Hard so Enjoy What You Do

When out and about, at a social gathering, at a dinner, at the beach, at your child's sports event, or anywhere where we come across people, someone will mention that life is hard. "No kidding Brian/you don't say Sheila".

We all know this. Life has trials, problems, suffering and hard times no matter who you are, how much money you have, how old you are, or what sex you are. None of us are excluded. If this is the case, why don't we choose to follow that dream we have? What do we have to lose?

Will it be tough at times? Yes. Will we doubt ourselves along the way? Yes. Will we feel like giving up sometimes? Yes. The fact remains that even if we never chased our dream and took a chance on what we really value or are passionate about, life will still be hard. Perhaps we should do the things we love to do then.

We are on a journey and along the way in the midst of family and laughter and opportunities, holidays, special moments, we will face trials. We can't escape it. But we do get to choose what we do, so take a step in that direction.

Reflect:

Do you know that you are not alone in facing your challenging situations?

Could you make a change to do something you enjoy?

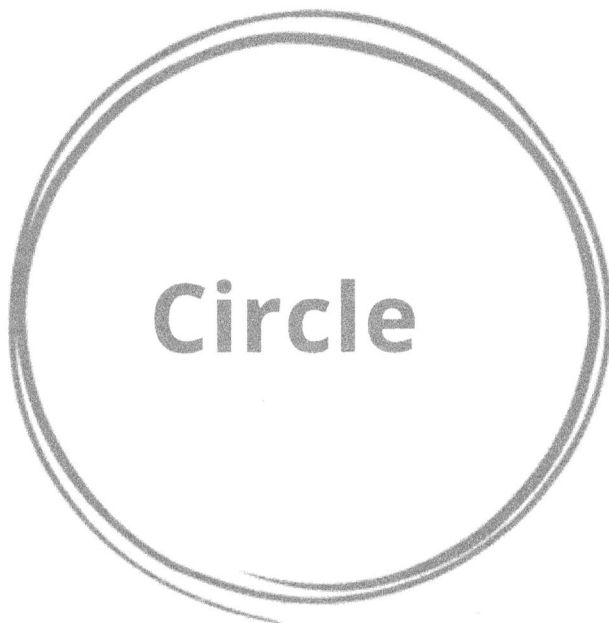

Circle

Understand

Have you ever been through a struggle of some kind and you meet with a well-meaning friend who says to you: "I understand what you are going through?"

I believe that when, for example, we lose someone we love, we can understand some of what the person experiencing grief is feeling, but not exactly.

Two people can experience the same thing differently. Be it a cocktail at the same restaurant, a cruise, a promotion, a demotion, the loss of a friend, a breakup, we all process things in our own way.

We are all unique and have our own upbringing, genes, and beliefs. There is no possible way that we can understand exactly what another person is experiencing.

We can be sad for someone but not experience the exact sadness they feel. We can be happy for someone we love but not as happy as they feel. It is good to accept this and let our friends and loved ones off the hook. Instead of saying, "You don't understand," perhaps we should wonder why we expect them to. They are there, they are listening, and they are supporting us. They don't have to understand or feel our exact pain or disappointment.

Reflect:

Can you adjust your expectations?

Can you appreciate support and not always understanding?

Love Gets Close

Not everyone is easy to love. We have family members whom we don't understand, co-workers who have ulterior motives, parents who hurt us over and over again, friends who betray us, and the list goes on.

We can also do seemingly kind actions that are backed up with empty emotions, having no love at the core of the intention.

The Bible says that we can prophesy and speak in the tongues of angels but if we don't have love we have nothing (1 Corinthians 13). We can do all the good deeds in the world but if we begrudge doing it, there's no point in doing it at all. God sees our heart and it's not that He catches us out like this, He just knows. And so do we.

To really know someone is to spend time with them. To perhaps be inconvenienced a few times. To be patient. To care enough to listen.

I see this in action when I watch my children with my elderly mother. They love spending time doing crosswords with her, listening to her stories, but more likely her listening to theirs. They walk slowly with her, laugh at her jokes, and help her with things in her house. They get close enough to know her. This is what love does.

Reflect:

Who do you battle to love?

24

Don't Show Me, Tell Me

Much of our behaviour involves trying to communicate to others how we feel about something, even if we aren't aware of it. Tantrums, eating disorders, self-harm, substance abuse and other behaviours are all ways in which we communicate how we feel.

What if we find the courage to use our voice? Could we tell others how we feel instead of showing them? It takes courage, it's brave and bold but it's worth the effort. The surprising thing is that when I have told someone how I feel, it usually opens a door for them to tell me how they feel, and it empowers both of us.

Telling someone how you feel is heroic, sharing feelings isn't for the faint hearted. The ego says that we don't have to say anything. It's easier not to. It's hard to be open. It takes work to be vulnerable. It takes strength.

Reflect:

Were there any instances today where you showed someone how you felt by what you did, when you could have perhaps spoken to them?

Do you have the courage to handle it differently next time?

What would you say?

Improve or Approve?

We spend time trying to improve ourselves. Whether it is how we look, behave, talk, or spend our time, we seek to do things better. Most of what we buy is always for improvement. Applications always need updating due to more advanced features, and almost everything around us sells because it has improved upon the previous version.

As parents, sometimes we want to improve our children. We try to improve their manners, their grades, or their behaviour. This can become tiring and tedious. Although we want children who are liked, we often try to improve them as if they were not the imperfect beings that we know *we* are.

What if we complimented our children on how they try to clean their room, on how they make a sandwich, or how they attempt to make us something special or brush their hair? As they grow, they will watch us and learn the more improved way anyway. Let's give our children some encouragement for those things that they do that may not be perfect but show great effort.

God loves us exactly as we are. He can see where we need improving and He will help us along the way, but it is His unconditional love that leads to our wanting to change. He doesn't nag.

Reflect:

Could you acknowledge peoples' efforts before jumping in to improve on what they are doing?

Honesty

The Bible says in Colossians 3:9 that we are not to lie to each other. Why is it so hard to be honest?

Maybe we are afraid of others' responses to our honesty. So instead, with our words we say "I'm fine", but we say "I'm not fine" by our actions. Overeating, over drinking, sleeping too much, feeling depressed, can be examples of how we act out, when we cannot admit that we aren't fine. This is our way of getting it out.

Think about your day today. Did you turn to any of these things instead of honestly facing what was going on? We meet for coffee or chat in the school car park telling each other how fine we are, how great our husbands/wives are doing, how well our children are performing, when often it's nothing like that at all, so we go home and act out. The funny thing is that we aren't even aware that we do it.

What do you need to honestly face in your life right now? Pushing the feeling away doesn't help you deal with it. Look at it and accept it is there. It then loses power.

Reflect:

Are you fine? Really?

It's okay not to have it all together. Give yourself permission not to be fine all the time.

Before You Say I Do

The Bible says that we should not stir up romantic love until the time is right (Song of Solomon 8:4).
Do we really need a mate to complete us or make us happy? There is so much to who we are. We have our passions, hobbies, friends, pets, family, careers, places of travel and wonderful, interesting people to meet. We can be happy without having a boyfriend/girlfriend or husband/wife, but if we choose to share our life with someone it is our choice, not something we do from society's endless question "When are you going to settle down?"

Be ready to get married. Do it when you are ready, not when you think your biological clock is running out or out of pressure from the special person in your life. The truth is, marriage is a commitment and we need to be equipped to take that step. An exciting adventure awaits you when you are ready.

Reflect:

Is there someone in your bed next to you? Look at him or her. Take a moment to appreciate this person and fall asleep reminding yourself why you are together.

If no one is sleeping next to you, spread out a little and enjoy the space!

Angry?

Perhaps today, something or someone made you angry. Take a moment to review your day. Did something happen that you didn't expect and that made you irritated or upset?

Being angry can be productive when directed in the right way. The Bible says in Ephesians 6:12 that our battle is not against flesh and blood but against powers and principalities. What does this mean? I'm no expert, but I think it hints that as people we are all flawed. We all have been through things that not everyone knows or understands. Half the time we don't understand why we behave like we do.

So perhaps we should be patient with each other and get angry at situations, incidents and injustice, but not aim it at a person. What is going on behind a person causes them to act in certain ways. Their upbringing, their mental state, their emotions, their past hurts all play a part.

Look beyond the person who made you angry, admit that you don't know everything about them.

Reflect:

Would you consider that the person who recently made you angry isn't perfect?

How Do We Trust?

We sometimes find it hard to trust others because we have been hurt in the past in one way or another.

Or perhaps we trust too easily and too soon rather than allowing time to pass to get to know someone before we let them in on our life story.

If someone tells you intimate details about someone else, chances are they will tell your story too, so tread lovingly with care.

When someone shares something and we listen attentively and don't tell others what they have said, slowly they begin to realize that we are trustworthy.

I think that it is okay to have only a few people that you really trust in life, those to whom you can tell everything and anything. Those who sincerely want what is best for you and who have your interests at heart.

Reflect:

Take time before you go to sleep to express gratitude for those close to you whom you trust.

Believe In Each Other

As a teacher, I love interacting with my students. It is a privilege when they let you into their life.

I recall one student saying to me that his father didn't believe in him. He told me, "He is just one of those parents who don't believe in their children." He quickly added, "But it doesn't bother me. I will prove him wrong." I looked at this young man and my heart was heavy. Who wouldn't believe in him? With his bright eyes and his kind heart, having a plan for his own future. How many of our parents believed in us? If they didn't, how did it impact us as we were growing up?

Let's choose to believe in each other, the opposite choice has no positives. If we fail when someone believed in us, it is better than failing and being told it was going to happen anyway. As parents, if we think our children are embarking on things that may not work out, let's at least be in their corners to support them while they try. We are afraid for them in case they do fail, but it's still better to believe in them on the way.

We have the greatest supporter of all time, Jesus, who is on the sideline - our cheerleader from heaven. He never stops believing in us.

Reflect:

Know that you have One who believes in you no matter what.

If there is someone next to you in bed, make a choice to believe in them too.

33

Atticus Finch

In the book *To Kill a Mockingbird*, Atticus Finch is the father of the main character, Scout, a young girl who narrates the story. After reading this novel, I realised that all the families in the book are parented by a single father. Why did the author Harper Lee do this? As you slow down and get ready for bed tonight, something from this timeless classic is worth noting.

Parenting influences our children, no matter how much we don't want to admit it. In the book we have three fathers. First, there is Atticus, who is a just and fair man who treats his children with respect and honesty. Secondly, there is Walter Cunningham who is very poor, but clean and well-mannered, as are his children. Thirdly, we have Bob Ewell who is a drunk and a liar, and who physically abuses his children, Bob's daughter lies in court which leads to the killing of an innocent man.

These three fathers left their imprint on their children--not by what they told their children to do, but by who they were every day in their dealings with their family.

Reflect:

Do you have or want children?

Could you decide to treat your children and family with respect and kindness even when you disagree?

Friends

No relationship can get stronger without time spent together. Whether it is time in person or online for some who live apart, we need time in each other's presence for a relationship to grow.

Do you know someone who complains about not having friends? Is that person a friend? Do they make time in their week for others? We can't make it a rule since we have commitments, but if we don't make time for getting together with friends, we won't have any.

One thing that has helped me is including friends in what I enjoy doing. If I am going for a walk, sometimes I will ask a friend along. If you like to do a certain activity, why not try every third time to ask someone to come along?

Try to think out of the box when it comes to seeing people. Asking a friend to collect you from the airport allows you to catch up, makes them feel valued and saves on taxi money. People like to feel needed, it's okay to ask for favours.

Reflect:

Think of something you have planned for tomorrow.

Could you invite a friend along?

Eating Together

Eating together as a family is something that all books and courses tell us to do for family bonding and communication. Do we really get to do it?

When the children are small and messy, it serves two purposes as we don't want our furniture ruined. As children get older and our lives get busier, we all come home at different times and often eat while watching the favourite series on TV.

Some people eat out a lot – no one has to cook or clean up and everyone gets to choose what they feel like. And if you can make a rule about no phones, you are generally in for a good evening.

When my son was home from a trip, he came out with his grandmother and me for Mexican food. Wow, I remembered who my son was that night. He told us all about his experiences overseas, was an absolute gentleman and we all had the most rewarding evening. It was relaxed, no rules (except I fall asleep at 9pm but we went early). It got me thinking how having a meal bonds us in ways that we cannot explain, and I think it has been going on for centuries.

Reflect:

Could you make it a priority once this week to sit with someone special in your life and have a meal with no distractions? It can even be eggs on toast!

Society

We can't get away from the fact that we live in a society. Even when we try to escape it, the place we run to has a society; and if we had to live there, we would become immersed in another society. I have battled with society's rules and standards and have tried to escape them many times. What if we can escape but still live in it? We can't all pack up and go and live in the mountains.

Some psychologists believe that our true nature and society are opposing forces and that a third entity exists to makes peace between the two.

Our true nature likes to take risks and longs for freedom. These urges seem to be constricted by the hidden standards and regulations that society deems correct. Perhaps it's more about finding how we can still be our authentic selves and yet live in a society.

God created us all to be unique individuals, to live honestly and authentically. Let's try and do it. Let's try and see our worth no matter what our bank balance is. Let's try and see beauty no matter what social media says. Let's try and love with sincerity no matter what television shows portray love to be. Choose you, choose God, and we may even see society change because of it.

Reflect:

How do you feel about society's norms?

Grandparents

How do you feel as you read the title above? We all have our own story with our own grandparents, or we are grandparents ourselves. If you are like me, it brings a sense of slowing down. Grandparents never seem to be in a hurry (maybe it's because they can't move quickly). Whatever the reason, there seems to be a patience about them as they walk their grandchildren into school, as they listen to the stories of the family, as they spend time cooking our favourite meal.

In some cultures, grandparents are esteemed and admired, whereas sadly, in other cultures, they are regarded as unintelligent and are admitted into homes where they are sometimes visited on weekends or forgotten altogether.

It is a beautiful thing to see how a grandparent looks at their grandchildren. They see pass the faults, the school marks, and the mistakes made. Whether it's ice cream for breakfast or late bedtimes, there are certain privileges for grandparents that shouldn't be taken away.

Reflect:

Could you decide to honour any grandparent of yours still living?

If you are a grandparent, know that you are valued and admired.

May a smile form on your lips as you fall asleep.

Don't Tell

We rely on external praise and validation more that we think. We all feel good when we give or help, and I think that's pretty normal. It's just an interesting exercise to do something for someone and not say anything about it to anyone (for a year).

It's a challenge I am going to try and since I am writing this entry in November 2021, I will see if I can seek out someone to help anonymously and then not tell a soul.

In the Bible there is a scripture that talks about people praying in the busy streets where everyone can see them. Jesus tells us to go into our room and close the door and pray in private where no one can see us and there we will receive our reward. Those that pray in the busy streets with everyone watching already have their reward in the people's admiration.
(Matthew 6:5)

Think of someone you can bless with your time/money/google review/anything you can think of and commit to do it and not say anything to anyone about it. You won't regret it.

Reflect:

Do you like people to see you do good things?

The Person (Not the Task)

We all have so much to get done each day. These tasks often require dealing with people (not just our checklist). Then sometimes people ask us to do certain favours or jobs for them. Do you ever feel like people's requests make you want to run in the opposite direction?

An ex-colleague reached out to me for help. I had left the job after being overwhelmed and burnt out. My first reaction to her request was dread. I paused, and committed to half of what she was asking me to do. Even that kept me up with night sweats. When praying the next morning, God showed me that if I saw it as helping a person, of meeting someone new and dealing with a fellow human being, I would be fine.

I saw the situation in a new light. I would maintain a healthy boundary but also see the person on the other side of the phone. It changed my perspective. Sadly, I still couldn't do it. I hope that shows you I am far from perfect.

Could we notice the people behind the task?

Reflect:

As you fall asleep tonight, could you decide to notice the people that you engage with each day while completing your tasks?

Forgiveness

Almost every book you read, or therapy session you attend, the topic of forgiveness will arise. It comes up time and again because we are all connected to one another. We interact and hurt each other and need to forgive each other.

Forgiving those who have apologised can seem reasonable but what about those who don't deserve our forgiveness? What about those who show no remorse for how they have affected our lives? The truth is they are sleeping well at night, and we are the ones tossing and turning, reliving the hurt they have caused.

Forgiveness doesn't mean that you must socialise or interact with that person again. It merely means letting go and setting yourself free from the influence that they have on your life.

A method I use is to picture the person in my mind and then say, "I choose to forgive ….. for what he/she did, and I let him/her go, he/she has no hold on me anymore". Note the word "choose" as it is not a feeling but a choice. You don't need to let the person know either, and you may not feel different right away but slowly as time passes you will feel lighter, more at peace and your heart will be softer; and that is the fruit of forgiveness.

Reflect:

Can you recall any person you feel you may have resentment towards?

Could you try to forgive them?

Change Someone?

We all do it, we judge people in the traffic, at work or school, on holiday, in the supermarket line or wherever we find ourselves. While invigilating an exam one day, I decided to look at the students one by one. (This was not the time I tried to match each of them with an animal!) Invigilating can be really boring!

I realised that I judged my students on how they engaged in class, their attitudes, their hair, and other superficial reasons that somehow justified how I felt about them. As they quietly wrote their exams, all trying their best, I realised that I knew so little about them. What was going on at home? What were their passions and their dreams?

Think about the people you have come across in your day today. Without giving it much thought, you may have judged them by some criteria without knowing them at all.

We all have bad days. We all have things going on that are our own personal struggles that we keep to ourselves.

Reflect:

Could you decide to judge less and accept more, to practise more patience and kindness?

Toxic People

Be it a boss, colleague, friend, acquaintance, employee, trainer—you name it—toxic people exist. The thing about toxic people is that they don't introduce themselves by saying, "Hi, nice to meet you. I am toxic. I will manipulate you and play on your emotions; and as I get to know you better, I will often play the victim and try to control you by any means possible. And what you do will never be good enough. Just so you know. Oh, my name is Carol" (no offense if your name is Carol).

Toxic people appear to be full of compliments, they want to be your friend and help you where they can. It's later that you get that sinking feeling that you want to say no but have to say yes. That you think about what you should have said but didn't say it.

How do we deal with these people? Jesus loves them. We are not perfect. Perhaps some of us are toxic. What are we to do?

I know that in my life I have had to remove myself, even if it meant leaving my job. Where my heart says one thing and my mouth another, I know I am in danger. When you have confronted, tried all you know how, loved and put-up boundaries and nothing works - get out.

Pray for toxic people (from a distance). I like to imagine the toxic person as a child and then pray for them as it helps me to see them in a different light.

Reflect:

Are you entwined in a toxic relationship of any kind?

Fathers

In my experience, most people have issues with their fathers. If you don't, you are one of the lucky few. We want our father's approval growing up and whether we get it or not doesn't stop us from trying. A father is supposed to protect and take care of us but often none of these needs are met.

Think about your father tonight as you go to sleep. Perhaps he has passed on or perhaps you haven't been in contact for a while, and you have been meaning to call.

Could you have the conversation with him that you keep putting off? Perhaps take the child-father roles away and just relate to him soul to soul with no judgement but just an acknowledgment that you don't know everything about how he was brought up or what he endured.

Reflect:

Rest knowing that your Father in heaven loves you unconditionally and He watches over you and protects you and is always there.

If you can't make that call to your dad, try and pray a blessing over your father as you doze off.

Touch

Most of us know the importance of physical touch. There are numerous studies showing how babies need physical touch to survive. It is often a love language we can tap into. I know that if I tickle my eldest son's back and not say a thing, we are bonding.

It seems that when our children are young, or our love is young, we give so many cuddles and tickles and then later in the relationship or when our children become teens, we lessen our physical contact when in fact they need it more than ever.

Whether tickling their back, giving hugs, a head massage, a back rub, a fun wrestling match, a foot rub, a gentle touch on the arm, find what works and do it. Not everyone wants to be held close, but we all need touch and it comes in so many forms.

Reflect:

Think about when you last touched those you loved and tomorrow try to touch them in some way.

If you are sharing a bed with someone, roll over now and give them a hug, or just touch their arm.

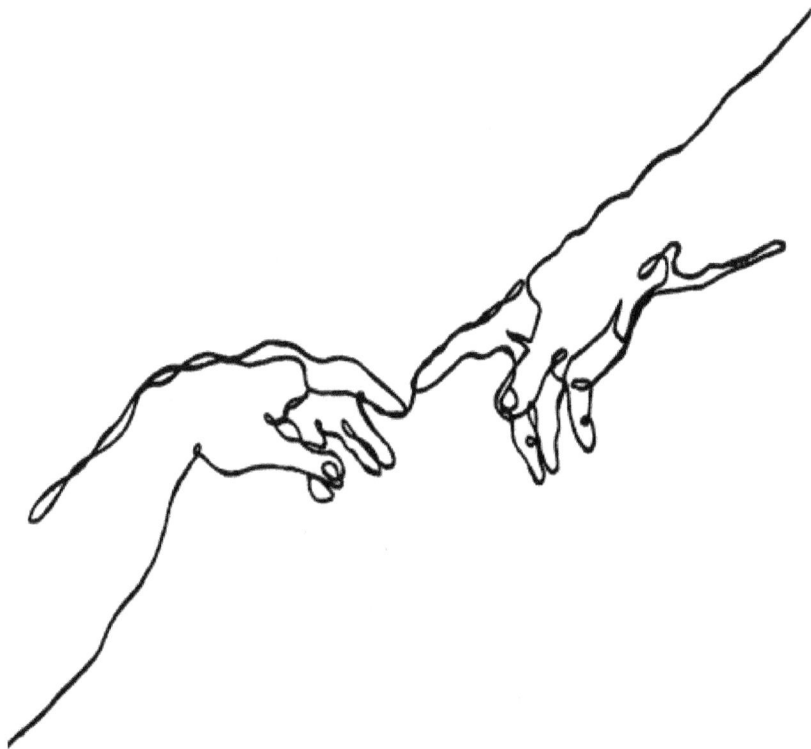

Living

49

Simple Living

A simple life clears the path for thought and balance in our lives. It sounds like something that is easy to grasp but it has taken me a long time to make it real in my life. I am still far from getting it right.

Simple living. We can't all be monks and retreat to a serene mountain to meditate and live the core of simplicity. But we can live simply if we make it a priority. Cleaning out our cupboard and getting rid of clothes we don't wear is a move towards a simpler life. Tidying the living area and decluttering where we do life is a move towards a simpler life.

Saying no to some invitations and saying yes to a few you really want to go to is a move towards a simpler life. Deciding and sticking to it is a move towards a simpler life.

I don't want to overcomplicate things. The more we have the more complicated life gets. The more technology we have, the more time we spend on it. The more possessions we have the more we must maintain them.

Reflect:

Are there ways in which you could simplify your life?

Less Drama

Have you ever had the experience where you read something, and certain words literally stand out in bold and almost jump out at you? This is where the title for this entry comes from. Instead of my usual route on a morning run, I felt to go a little further instead of going down the hill as I usually did. I thought it must be the shade that attracted me, and I carried on.

I came across a few real estate boards that were pegged in the ground and the words "Less Drama" stood out and "came" towards me. For one thing, I have never seen a real estate board that ever mentioned these two words. I had seen "sold", "for sale", "we are the best" but never the words "Less Drama". God was showing me something.

Do we add drama to situations? We pretend that we know what others think about us and we create drama that isn't even true. We add juicy bits into our stories of why we were hard done by and at times, if we're honest, we could audition for a role in our own play. Could we be less dramatic? Is it necessary to let everyone know the lengths to which you go?

Reflect:

Do you know anyone who is often dramatic? How do you feel around them?

Do you tend to be dramatic? Could you change this?

Done Versus Perfect

Can you finish something and be happy with "good enough" or does it have to be flawless? Is it okay to get something done and not aim for perfection? What about excellent work ethics and standards? It can depend on what the task is. I don't want to go in for an operation and the surgeon does a "good enough" job on me!

However, there are times when our pedantic and perfectionistic tendencies can get in the way. I have worked with a perfectionist boss, and it wasn't fun. As staff, we felt like we could never meet her expectations. There were always corrections to our work, and it didn't do much for the morale of the employees.

If you are a perfectionist, could you take a deep breath and try do something until it is "good enough" and let go of the control to check every detail to the point that it does no good? Giving others the freedom to fail and learn from their mistakes takes courage, even when you know that you could do it better yourself. The pressure of producing perfect work all the time and being the perfect person having the perfect body is a standard that is unattainable.

Not one person in the world is perfect. This gives us grace to be ourselves and know that who we are is okay. When you come across as perfect or even mention your standards of perfection, it can leave others feeling like they are not good enough.

Reflect:
Do you tend to want everything to be done perfectly?

Numbers

While on another run (I wish I still ran as often!) on a beautiful road that overlooks the ocean, I started to notice the numbers of the houses I passed. Then I saw telephone numbers on the posters tied to the electricity poles, then a car drove pass, and I noticed the number plates. I started to think about numbers. The Bible tells us in Matthew 10:30 that God even knows the number of hairs that we have growing on our head.

Sometimes we feel like a number, like we aren't seen. We each have a name given to us at birth. Yet we judge our worth by numbers. The numbers in our bank account, the model number of the car we drive, the number of assets we own. We go to university, and we are given a student number, we have an employee number, our rankings in sports are all about numbers.

We do need numbers to make sense of the world, but perhaps we could be aware of not treating each other based on numbers. Each of us is unique, with our own fingerprint, our own strengths and weaknesses, our own giftings and talents. God works with numbers but in a different way than the world does. God does not base his love or approval on any number system.

Reflect:

Are there areas in your life where you feel like just a number?

How many things in your life are controlled by numbers? Where can you bring a more personal touch to dealing with others?

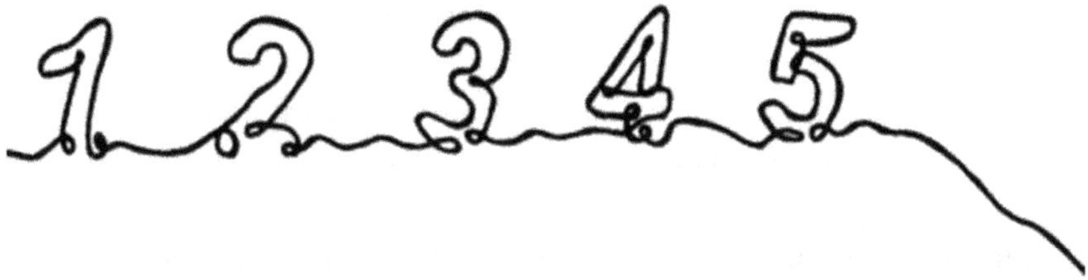
1 2 3 4 5

Just Visiting

According to the Bible, our home is in heaven, that is where our citizenship is (Philippians 3:20). We are in the world but not of the world. What does this mean? Perhaps a personal story can make the point a little clearer.

At the time of writing this, we rent a home in Umdloti, South Africa. I had always wanted to own a home. Then one day when I was spending some alone time in God's presence, I saw my home in heaven, like I was looking at a photograph. It is set on the bank of a hill in a small bay. The house is wooden and high up. It looks beautiful. I didn't get to see inside, I guess some things are worth waiting for. This was a very clear vision for me. It dawned on me, that my home is in heaven.

I am just visiting earth for now and one day I will be at home, my true home, with my Saviour, Jesus and my Papa, God the Father.

I have visited places before in my life and I am amazed at how few clothes I need and how we can all stay in a small cabin with one bathroom and a tiny kitchen. And we love it!! So, if we are visiting earth and our home is in heaven, maybe we don't need as much as we think we do. Things are temporary here where we are visiting. There is no point storing up for us everything we can when there are those in need and we can help them.

Reflect:

How would you approach life differently if you embraced the concept that heaven is your true home?

Culture

Without searching the definition of the word "culture", if we pause and look at it, it has the word "cult" in it. We accept that culture may be our customs and traditions depending on where we live and yet it is also the thinking patterns of a certain group of people.

The word is derived from the Latin word "cultura" which means growing or cultivation. When we say, "That's part of our culture" to explain a certain behaviour pattern that may be foreign to others, do we stop and think about it? Can culture change? Is culture the same as traditions? Does culture involve religion? Are we locked into our culture? What was the culture of Jesus and the early disciples?

What idols does our culture portray? Self-centeredness? Selfishness? Ambition? Do we belong to a cult of putting ourselves first no matter what the cost? If so, do we want to be a part of our culture?

What about cultural practices that cause harm and pain? Do we justify these and put it down to something that can't be changed? Chinese women used to have their feet bound in bandages to make them smaller. This painful and physically deforming practice doesn't happen much anymore. Someone thought it wasn't right and challenged having their feet broken in the name of society's rules and standards.

Reflect:

Is there anything in your culture that you would like to see change?

What do you buy into without realising it?

We Don't Have to Make It Up

We are not stumbling along in life alone, walking or tripping forward toward our destiny. God says that we are His handiwork, created in Christ Jesus to do good works, which God prepared in advance for us to do (Ephesians 2:10).

There was a time in my life where I had left a job that I know God wanted me to leave and I thought that something would come along straight away. It didn't happen. I applied for so many positions and ... nothing. I then went to a friend for prayer who shared truth with me from the Bible. She encouraged me, saying that God wanted me to rest in the season I was in, and I was not to worry as He did have things for me to do. He prepared these things in advance for me, and I would do them when He thought I was ready.

What a burden was lifted from me that day! I decided to rest in the knowledge that God's Spirit would lead me in applying for the right job as there is work for me to do. I haven't been left out of His master plan. How peacefully I slept after that.

Reflect:

As you drift off to sleep tonight, rest in the knowledge that God has something for you to do. He has knitted this special task into your DNA.

Seek Him and wait on Him. Let His wonderful plan for you unfold.

Nothing Wasted

Do you find that the areas in your life where you have battled the most is where God ends up using you? When we have been through something, experienced something for ourselves, we empathize with those going through the same thing. It is true that we can't help someone when we are at our lowest point emotionally, but in time and with the lessons that we learned from the experience, we can be there for those going through similar circumstances.

If we were perfect/qualified/experts, how could we ever relate to others facing struggles?

Jesus was found among the sick, poor, and wounded. Where do we find ourselves? Among the well, rich and whole people?

It's okay not to have it all together, it's okay to need help and healing, it makes us human. It's our wounds and not our giftedness that qualifies us.

Reflect:

Could you share with someone going through a hard time?

Could you be honest about your struggles?

Detach

The Bible says that a person who detaches his life from this world and abandons himself to Jesus, will find true life and enjoy it forever (John 12:25).

What does detach mean and how do I detach from a world that I live very presently within? Detach means to separate from, disconnect, disengage from, pull away, dissociate with. We can't all take a week off and go and stay in a deserted cabin in the woods and alienate ourselves from the world.

So, what does the Bible mean? I certainly don't have all the answers but when God challenged me with this, I began to reflect on ways in my life that were in allegiance to the world rather than to God's ways. For example, seeing people differently based on what they do. The world says we are more important if we have a successful career. God does not. I can change this perspective. How? By treating every person with the same care and attention no matter who they are.

Another example that challenged me was my appearance. As we age, our bodies change, our hair turns grey, and we look "more experienced". Being married to a man nine years my junior adds to my challenge. To accept that God sees my heart, my wrinkles, and my wobbly bits, and says that I am beautiful is so freeing. I can do the best with what I have and then accept who I am.

Reflect:

What are some of the practices you take part in every day? Is there anything in your life you feel you could adjust?

Response Time

How quick are you to respond? Do you drop everything to answer emails, missed calls and messages?

I find that when I respond too quickly, I often regret my response.

I am not talking about the usual messages from family and loved ones that happen daily, or an emergency situation. Rather I am talking about messages and mails that require a decision of some sort – whether it's an invite for dinner, a request for help/money/time or something similar.

One morning, after responding to a message efficiently and quickly and then regretting it, I felt like God showed me something. He gave me a window period – to wait a day to respond to such messages. This gives me time to think about it, to pray about it and to see the situation or request from all angles before responding. I even discuss it with my husband in the evening and when I respond, it is with truth and sincerity. The best thing about doing this consistently is that people soon catch on that you don't respond straight away, and they stop expecting you to.

Reflect:

Could you let go of pressure to respond to all messages straight away?

Small Beginnings

"Don't despise small beginnings" – we know this saying. So many stories we hear about successful people involve starting a business in the garage or from their bedroom and how slowly it grew over time.

Nowadays we want everything instantly, including success. We all know that a healthy eating plan takes a while to work. If we lose weight too quickly, we put on even more than before. Most things take time to work, success requires patience, perseverance, courage, stamina and all those good character-building things that mold us into better people.

As you fall asleep tonight, allow your mind to drift and think about that thing that you always wanted to do but thought that it would never work. Think about the possibility that it could work. We don't have to leave our job, but just start small with an idea. Work at it slowly and watch what happens.

Reflect:

Can you pick up that idea again and take one small step to make it happen?

Place

We know that certain places are famous for certain things. When I travelled to India, my friend took me to a famous restaurant in Mumbai called Leopold's. If you have ever read the book "Shantaram" this restaurant will be familiar to you. If you haven't read the book, go, and buy it tomorrow!

Sitting in Leopold's in Mumbai with slow ceiling fans, bullet holes in the walls, (very old holes!) sipping warm beer and eating butter chicken curry with naan bread surrounded by international people and many beautiful Indian customers, was an experience I will never forget.

I could take you to our local restaurant in South Africa where I live and order a butter chicken curry but it's not going to have the same impact as going to Leopold's in India for their famous dish. **Place matters.**

Where you are matters. Making memories matters. What places impacted you as a child? Take your children there and show it to them. What places have been important experiences for you? Revisit them when you can. Take trips to different places. It doesn't have to cost a lot. Take a walk down the road you live on with a family member and create a memory about the road, the flowers, pick them and put them in a vase. And do it again next week.

Reflect:

As you fall asleep think about where you used to go as a child, the places that make you nostalgic, the foods and smells, and its pace.

Give One Away

In the Bible Jesus says that by giving to those in need, we make deposits in heaven and that these gifts for us are secure and last forever (Luke 12:33).

When we give on earth, we make a deposit in heaven. We know that our home and final destination is heaven. We will be there forever. It stands to reason that it would make more sense to have deposits in the place where we will spend the most time. Life on earth is a lot shorter than our time in heaven, so as we give here on earth, we receive treasure in heaven.

Does this mean that we must sell all we have and give it away? Or do we perhaps have two of something, and we could give one away?

God honours our small steps. Perhaps if we have bought new shoes, we could give an older pair away. We could start small by supporting a volunteer organisation in our area. When our hearts are open to give, we don't have to seek out people who are in need, they often will come across our path. Yes, we may have to be aware and cross the road to get to them, but we will see them.

Reflect:

Do you have two of anything?

Could you give one away?

No Lyrics

When last did you listen to a piece of music with no lyrics? With no words to guide you to the singer's thoughts, the music itself allows your brain to engage in a different way. Your imagination lights up, memories come rushing in.

We can even make up our own story to the music. Usually, it involves us in some way! We can add our own words to the song or simply allow our mind to wonder and feel a stillness that words don't allow us. A melody can give us peace of mind. The sound of birds or a stream creates its own melody too, as nature knows how to compose without words.

Sometimes I love the tune of a song and then the lyrics leave me wishing they had kept quiet as I scroll to find a song that fits my mood.

Reflect:

Could you listen to one piece of music this next week that has no words?

Life Lessons

How often do we bump into people randomly during the day or think about someone we haven't seen for a while? If we take a moment to slow down and think about it, we realise that God was using that person to teach us something or to show us something.

In South Africa we have car guards who watch your car when you go to shop/park at the beach or park anywhere for that matter. Often, the kindest smile of the car guard is the only genuine smile I see all day. It's God, connecting with me through this human being, humbly and quietly watching my car for me.

I want to be aware of these opportunities to learn things from unlikely places. Often, I am so busy that I miss them.

Reflect:

Could you decide to notice the small things tomorrow? A smile, a sunrise or sunset, a pretty butterfly, a breaking wave, a kind gesture, a laugh, a cry, or anything He chooses to catch your attention.

Let God show you that we are all connected and all loved.

Wonder

If you have ever read a fairy-tale to a young child and noticed their facial expressions at the delight and wonder of the story, you will know what I am talking about here. As we grow older, we can lose our sense of wonder.

Childbirth – what a wonder! When you first fell in love, when your child got married, when you felt God's unconditional love for the first time and every time since - the sense of wonder.

I don't want to lose my sense of wonder at who God is and how He works in my life. When I am asking Him something and He answers, when I pray for one of my children and He gives me a picture, when someone I love comes to know Him deeper, may I cherish the moment.

May we never lose our wonder.

Reflect:

As you fall asleep tonight, recall to mind something you asked God to help you with and remember his faithful response.

Take a deep breath and acknowledge the wonder of who He is.

Old Roads or Highways?

When driving to a distant place, do you seek out the quickest route via the highway or do you ever take the old road – the one that the local people used before the freeway was built? These roads meander, are often lined with trees and orchards lending themselves to a completely different experience.

When I was young, my dad would always choose the quickest route, it was about getting to where we were going. I married a man who likes to take the road less travelled, the scenic route, where the journey is part of the experience, not merely something to be rushed through to get to where we are going.

Travelling these roads introduces you to new sights. Whether it be the local people, farm stalls, firewood or friendly drivers. Farm smells assault your senses as you drive slow enough to open the car windows. The odds of discovering good coffee are high.

So, I guess the challenge is the next time you plan a trip, allow for an extra day so that you don't have to switch into robot mode until you reach your destination. Notice what is around you, take a detour, go on a new adventure, and see where it leads you. Adjust your thinking, it is good for you.

Reflect:

Did you try and get everything done today as quickly as possible? Could you have spent a little time with someone instead of rushing off?

Taking the Short Cut

On my way to work, I drive along a major highway and every now and again, a pedestrian makes a run for it, across the freeway. One morning, a pedestrian nearly lost his life, and a few weeks prior to that a person did. It was tragic. It couldn't be undone. If these people walked a little further to the pedestrian bridge and crossed the road where it was safe, although it takes a little longer, their lives would have been safer.

This may seem quite severe, but a truth hit home that day. Taking the short cut in our daily lives whether at work, or at home isn't necessarily the safer road.

The Bible teaches us that planning puts us ahead in the long run whereas hurry and scurry puts us behind (Proverbs 21:5). We often try and take the short cut in life in so many areas.

Making a quick buck in a dishonest way rather than working honestly and consistently is another example of taking a short cut. Money made easily and quickly never lasts.

At the time, we don't think about the long-term consequences as we are in a rush and we have other things on our mind. We assume it will all work out. Sometimes it does, but mostly doing something properly pays off.

Reflect:

Did you take any short cuts today? What were they?

Lesson from Bali

I had the privilege of being given a trip to Bali, Indonesia. All expenses were paid by parents of one of my students, no teacher's present can ever top that one!

My husband and I enjoyed two blissful weeks submerged in a new culture. We tasted different food and drinks and experienced the intense heat of the tropics.

It sounds cliché, but it's the people that make a place. The Balinese people stood out to us as kind and hard working. They were up so early, and their routines seemed mundane at times but there was a consistency to what they were doing, a type of rhythm. It got me thinking about the rhythm of my life. What are the predictable beats that fill my week, day in and day out?

We love living near the ocean and that is a rhythm that I cherish. Coffee with my husband before work where we act silly and discuss things is a rhythm. My relationship with God, our talks and prayers and the way I lean on Him is a rhythm.

What are the rhythms of your life? What are the harmonious sounds? What rhythms bring you peace?

Reflect:

Can you make one small decision to adjust the rhythms of your life?

Pace

God challenged me with questions about pace one morning. What is my pace? Each day, what is my speed? Do I wake up in a panic, late for something? Do I start slow and then rush? Do I have time to notice the small, beautiful things around me or am I too busy?

Can I admit to being in control of the pace of my day? What is the rhythm I put out there? What is my stride like as I go about my day?

Then there is the verb part of the word "pace". Life isn't a sprint, it's more like a marathon and I need to pace myself. If I do some exercise in the morning, am I exhausted for the rest of the day? How do I pace myself? I tend to not eat and then I just about crash from being exhausted and then grab something sugary to lift me up. Not the best way to pace myself I admit.

Reflect:

Looking back on your day, what was the pace like? Was it a rushed day? Was it slow? How would you like to adjust tomorrow?

Allow the pace of your breathing to slow down and drift off to sleep.

Words Matter

There is a scripture that mentions how a bit in the horse's mouth is so small and yet it can control such a large beast. It then goes on to say that our tongues are like that – small but possessing immense power (James 3:3).

I like people who are sincere with their words. Insincere comments don't help anyone. Can we keep it real and hold our tongues? I told my children when they were young to ask the "TNK" question before speaking, i.e. is it True, Necessary and Kind? It must meet all three criteria to continue with what you want to say.

We can build others up with what we say. We can change someone's day based on what comes out of our mouths. Our words can break someone down or build them up; and in a matter of minutes, once the words are out, there is no taking them back.

Reflect:

What did you say today that built people up? Did you encourage someone with your words today?

If you used your words to criticise today, let it go and be more aware of your words tomorrow.

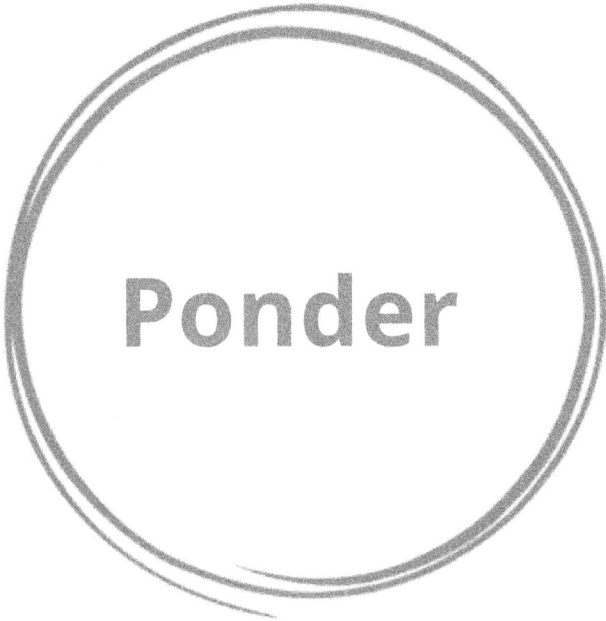

Ponder

Hold On?

We all have things in our lives that we hold on to. Things that we know are not particularly good for us, but we can't seem to break out of the cycle they create. For me, at the time of writing this, it's red wine! Yes, I know it's not a sin to drink red wine, even Jesus turned water into wine!

It's more like the hold it has on me, that I don't seem to be able to say no to having it. For some of us, it may be something we do when no one is looking. Be honest with yourself. Admit it and if you are brave enough, admit it to a friend too. Turn away from choices that are destructive.

We don't have to do this alone. God is closer than we think and so are the people in our lives who care about us. We just have to let them in.

Reflect:

What do you need to let go of?

What are you holding on to that is holding you back?

Master Mind

Our mind is useful to us but not as our master. The part of you who witnesses your thoughts is wisdom. Think about that for a moment. You are not your thoughts. How can you be if you are aware of what you are thinking? Who is that part of you behind your thoughts? This sets us free. We are not those ugly thoughts we think about someone, we are behind those thoughts.

We often make quick decisions. We get advice but fail to stop and be still and quiet. Quieten the mind and go within to the truth-telling voice. Check in with your intuition. Hear something deeply and get alignment. Don't rush decisions. It's a journey to learn to trust your inner voice. Trust your inner compass.

We often identify where we didn't trust our inner voice after something has happened. We look back at it and so we learn to trust the voice next time. Be kind and patient with your beautiful self, there's no rush.

Reflect:

Be aware of the real you, behind your thoughts and allow God to lead you to your core self.

You are good and beautiful in your innermost part.

One Purpose?

Many books claim that we all have one purpose in life and it's our goal to discover and pursue it. This is fine if you have known since a child that you wanted to be a social worker or an athlete and you have never strayed from that dream. But what about those who have talents and goals and dreams but can't pin it down to one thing? I see this in my two sons who love the ocean and have talents in and out of the water.

Telling someone that they have one purpose in life is too much pressure. God can use us no matter where we are or what we are doing. He isn't limited to us finding our life's calling so that He can use us. I once heard someone say that your job is something that we do where God uses you to love others.

There are times when we know we need to move on or change jobs but there are those who don't have the advantage of this decision due to poverty, lack of education or family dynamics. God can give you peace and purpose where you are right now. Let Him guide the promotion and the change.

Pursuing our one true calling can lead to disappointment, a feeling of failure and regret.

Reflect:

Could you embrace where you are right now?

Do you know that you are not alone in wanting something else?

Stress

Stress is the topic of conversation-the cause of so many illnesses and relationship breakups. With all the information available to us we have all the tools in the world to combat stress. Then why are we stressed more than ever?

Jesus said that His yoke is easy, and His burden is light (Matthew 11:30), which doesn't sound like a stressful life. I believe that herein lies the key. If we hand our burdens over to Him, He is capable of dealing with them. God knows what we need when we need it. He is a good father, not giving bad gifts to His children.

It is our need to be in control that is a large part of why we stress. We are never promised a life without trouble, but we do have the promise of help from a Father who loves us more than we can imagine.

Reflect:

As you fall asleep tonight, could you hand over your problems and challenges to God? He wants to help us; we are His children.

Sleep lighter knowing that the One who never sleeps has it all under control.

Age

One of my daughter's many qualities is the capacity to relate to people of all ages, from toddlers to grandparents, from teenagers to my friends in their 50's. She is never put off by the company she keeps, no matter who they are. I have watched her over the years engage with friends, acquaintances, teachers, family, and children with equal interest and empathy. She has taught me that age isn't what is important about a person. Rather, it is being in the presence of a precious soul, and our interaction with them. She genuinely listens and appreciates what they have to say and learns from every person she encounters.

Our bodies are our "clothes" worn by our true selves (our souls) while we are on earth, and yet we pay so much attention to these "clothes" without really taking note of what's on the inside. We may be missing out on experiences that could take our breath away by excluding interactions with certain people based on their age.

Do we shrug off the old man or lady we regularly pass by? The Bible tells us in Job 12:12 that wisdom is found in these people. What about the teenager who always looks angry?

Looking into another's eyes, whether walking pass each other on the street, teaching students in the class, smiling over coffee, or lingering on a date with a loved one, let's take time to notice each other.

Reflect:
Who did you interact with today? Do you treat people differently because of their age?

The Blanket

I find myself walking along sometimes with a "blanket" around my shoulders. I captured these thoughts through poetry:

The Familiar Blanket
Warm but stale and familiar,
Is my blanket I keep wrapped around my shoulders,
Its weight is a comfortable burden that holds
my patterned responses,
my preconceived ideas,
my past hurts,
my insecurities.

Lord, place Your foot on my blanket behind me and as I walk forward today,
Let it slip onto the floor,
Let me embrace all life has in a fresh way,
This lightness that holds
uncertainty yet adventure,
apprehension yet excitement,
freedom and expanded opportunities,
Will my courage resist the temptation to turn around and pick it up?

Reflect:

Could you choose to take your blanket off? Could this awaken you to new possibilities and ways of thinking and seeing?

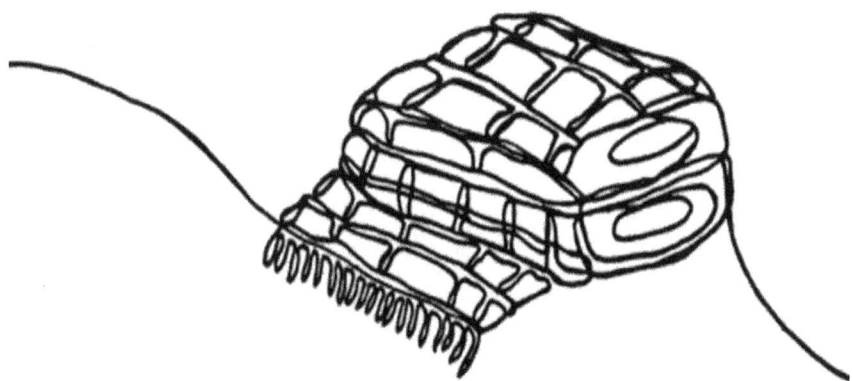

Meditation

This word has so many connotations. I used to think it was an eastern philosophical practice of shutting off your mind and chanting something in Sanskrit. Well, it can be that, but meditation to me is slowing my thoughts down and being consciously aware of where I am at a particular moment. When I read a verse in the Bible and contemplate it, I consider this meditating too.

As you get into bed this evening, I would encourage you to try for a few minutes to be aware of what you are thinking. Notice the thoughts as they pass through your mind. As already mentioned, you are not your thoughts. The presence that is aware of your thoughts is you. Meditation is getting in touch with that part of you behind your thoughts.

"Watch the traffic go pass, don't try and get into the traffic to stop it, you will get run over". So, it is with your thoughts, let them drift by but don't try to prevent them from coming.

Reflect:

As you become aware of your thoughts, notice the bed beneath your body, wiggle your toes, notice the sheets and your head on the pillow and acknowledge being alive. You got through today and tomorrow is another thing altogether.

Practise meditation as often as you can, sometimes it may involve thinking about a particular scripture that God has highlighted to you. Don't be in a rush to leave this space in your mind.

Security

This topic started brewing within me while I was telling God what I would do if I won the lottery. I then started to wonder about my sense of security. Money or God? Which is more powerful? Which one can change? Which is my anchor? Is it a large bank balance or trusting in a God I claim is a loving Father who only has good things planned for me? I began to ask Jesus to help me to rest in Him. I asked Him to help me not to long after a bank balance to feel secure. I had to be real.

Where does your trust lie? God? People? Money? You and your efforts? Can you really be content in any circumstances? These questions are tough and hard to answer honestly.

What is the secret to fully believing that no matter what, God is in control, is in charge, won't let us down, will provide all that we need and won't let us go hungry? There are so many questions. I am curiously and earnestly looking for some answers. One thing I find helps when I am in this place of questioning is to go to my room and shut the door, put on worship, and forget about it. If I can access God's presence and lift my eyes off the world, I gaze at His face and see Him for who He is. I remember that heaven is my home, and that this life is temporary and all has been okay in the past and it will continue to be in the future.

Reflect:

Could you remind yourself tonight that God is real, interested in the details of your life, and has got good things planned for your future?

Chains

I saw a picture of a chain when I was praying recently. It was a row of chain stitches of wool. (I admit I love to crochet!) Unsure of what it meant, I forgot about it. Later the same day my daughter sent me a picture of chain earrings saying that she knew that they would come in fashion. God was trying to tell me something. Both chains were quite delicate, so it ruled out "being in chains" as an interpretation.

I think it is to do with our interdependence and interconnectedness to each other. We rely on each other to draw strength. We know that a chain is strong unless broken. Whether we like it or not, we rely on and depend on one another, and we are affected by each other. We don't have to like this, but it is true.

We are affected by our environments and what surrounds us every day. There is a type of synergy that emerges when we link into our chains in life. Let go of what the word chain means in the negative sense and allow yourself to be strengthened by those around you. In turn, show compassion and grace to those you are near each day and watch what God can do.

Reflect:

Could you accept that you are not an island, and you are weaker alone?

Could you allow yourself to be part of the chain at work, at home, with friends or wherever you find yourself?

Surrender and Slow Down

I love the sound of this title for this evening's reading, although both are not as easy as one would think.

Surrender means that I give to God what I think is right, relevant, urgent, important, and let Him decide. In theory, I'm so for this, to relinquish responsibility and let God do it. Not as easy as it sounds, from someone who likes to be in control. But... dare to do it! God will never let us down; He knows best and His timing is perfect.

Slowing down is such an attractive action – moving in a way that is less frantic, less stressed, less manic. My husband told me once that if you do everything slower (talk, move, act, read), then people respond by slowing down and the pace of everything changes around you. I tried it at school one day and he was right! (he loves it when that happens)

Reflect:

As you drift off to sleep tonight, could you purpose to slow down tomorrow.

You will still get everything done but you may notice the important things too.

Slow those thoughts down right now and remember something that you love to do.

Doing Nothing

This title can either make you relax or make you judge me as being lazy. No matter what the response, science proves that doing nothing is good for you.

Moments of doing nothing – daydreaming, staring at the sea, walking through a forest, cloud gazing, lying under the shade of a tree, hanging out with your pets, bird watching from your bed – allow the brain to regenerate. Creativity starts to flow and new ideas to come to the forefront. It has been proved that solutions to ideas often come from periods of doing nothing.

(Scrolling through social media doesn't count as doing nothing!!) Taking a few moments in bed to put your phone down and lie there does count as doing nothing.

People equate busyness with importance, but this can also mean that they can't manage their time properly. The next time someone calls and asks you what you are doing, be brave enough to say, "Nothing". You get used to it; it is so liberating.

Reflect:

Revisit your favourite holiday, think about your family, or just try and hang out in your brain's nothing box before drifting off.

Plan A or B

Do you have a plan B for your life? No matter how old you are? I have always thought this was reasonable, realistic, and responsible. To have something to fall back on if what I really want to do doesn't work out.

I have changed my mind.

The more we know we have the safety net, the less we try. Subconsciously knowing that a friend will give us a job that we don't really enjoy but at least it will pay the bills isn't always a good thing.

You are you; you have things inside of you. Do what you do best. Fail and get up and fail and get up but keep going. Listen to podcasts of famous people who all tell their stories about their long road to become a success. It is possible and it's worth fighting for. It makes you come alive.

Reflect:

Allow the dreams you have to come to the surface.

Would you ask God to bring them back to life and to open doors and watch what happens?

Who Are You?

Wow, this seems like a loaded question! You know your name and where you come from. But do you know who you are?

You are first and foremost a child of God. Whether you believe it or not, it is true. You are a child, protected by a loving Father, who has a destiny and a future in mind for you.

You may not know what tomorrow holds, but there is One who does, who wants the best for you ALWAYS, and who never gives up on you.

He is not a man that He should lie. He is loving, patient, kind and very powerful. As a child trusts, so can we. As a child believes what his/her parents say, so can we. As a child doesn't worry and lives in the present moment with curiosity, so can we.

Reflect:

Think about the childlike qualities that you want to reclaim.

Could you decide to be more curious about life?

Could you do some silly, fun stuff and to be more trusting of your Dad in heaven?

You Don't Have to Be Poor to Be Holy

We don't often talk about this. There are people in the world with a lot of money who are good people. There are people who love God and worship Him, living godly lives who are extremely wealthy. We tend to think sometimes that people with a lot of money don't face any real hardships, or we wonder why they are not selling their possessions and giving the proceeds to the poor.

And then we go back to what God whispered in my ear: "You don't have to be poor to be holy". Secretly in our deepest thoughts, do we believe that a priest who owns nothing is holier than a person who has monetary wealth and serves God with the same passion and commitment?

If our business does well, we don't have to feel guilty about it. We can be grateful that God has blessed our business and blessed us with the talent to make money. What about the stay-at-home mom who doesn't work and seems to have a life of luxury? Yes, she too is just as holy.

We don't see every moment of anyone's lives, so we cannot make a judgement on how someone else spends their time. Perhaps that stay-at-home mom prays for her family and friends and her community for hours on end. Perhaps she gives time to reading to less fortunate children who are hungry for hope and the love of God. How she gets the time to do this is a mystery in itself.

Reflect:

Do you have preconceived ideas about certain professions?

Change?

Years ago I watched a movie about a group of surfers who went on an adventure - hiking and surfing waves in different locations around the world. While they were climbing a mountain there was a group of men who flew halfway up the mountain in a helicopter rather than climbing themselves. They still got to see the summit by only climbing the last part of the mountain.

The surfer being interviewed said, "The problem with being dropped halfway up the mountain is that if you were an asshole before climbing the mountain, you could still be an asshole when you came down, because being dropped off half of the way up does you no good."

It got me thinking that our character is often built in the "climb" of life. When we have to dig deep, it molds us and makes us into different people. If we just get "dropped off" and don't do the "climbing", we could be preventing our character from being shaped, preventing ourselves from growth.

Reflect:

Are you climbing a mountain of some sort in your life?

Could you accept that you have the strength, stamina, and support to climb it with God at your side?

Hiding

If you slowly recap what you did today and remember the people you saw, were you hiding behind anything?

Did you hide behind your makeup and hair style to conceal how you were really feeling? Did you hide behind anger when you really were feeling insecure? Did you hide behind your ego when you really were feeling afraid or not accepted? Did you hide behind being loud when you were really feeling alone?

We all hide behind something, and it is brave and vulnerable to try and take these fortresses down. Authentic living requires us to be sincere. It's amazing the effect it has on others. It's like we give others permission to be themselves and to know that it's okay.

Reflect:

Can you identify what you hid behind today?

Could you make a point of waking up without it tomorrow?

Regret

While walking on our local promenade, I felt a nudge inside me, like God said, "I want to chat about you know what." I told God that I didn't want to start crying and I wasn't ready to chat about it. He insisted and I sat down on a bench, watching the waves.

I had let go of something that happened in the past that I knew I could have prevented. I could not forgive myself. God started speaking to me through gentle thoughts that began to run through my head. It went something like this:

God: Maybe you didn't stop it, but I am more powerful than you and I didn't stop it either, so are you as cross with me as you are with yourself?

Me: Huh? No, I'm not cross with you. You are God and You are good. I just wish I could go back. She shouldn't have been there; it was my fault.

God: Why stop there, how far do you want to go back? If you hadn't got divorced, it wouldn't have happened. If you hadn't lived in Umdloti it wouldn't have happened. If you hadn't got married, it wouldn't have happened. I could go on…

Me: Thank you Papa. I will forgive myself.

Reflect:

Can you decide to forgive yourself for something you regret doing?

Nature

Beautiful Places

We all enjoy going away on holiday or experiencing a change in our surroundings. In 2016, as I mentioned previously in the book, I was lucky enough to be blessed with a trip to Bali, Indonesia. I recorded some of the sights, smells and sounds one evening. The purpose of the words below are to slow your thoughts down to encourage you to breathe and be aware of what is around you....

My journal entry from a day in Bali:

Ice blue water, white sand, white clean coral, warm water, cold Bintang beer, refreshing breeze, lazy days, outside showers, blue lagoon, cliffs, surfers, fresh fish and chips, sunburnt faces, four poster bed, aircon, satay sauce, gelato ice cream, bargaining at the market, iced coffee, Walter Mitty movie, ferry trip, friendly faces, children's smiles, scooters and taxis, sweet smells, rice, palm trees, temples, bamboo, money changers, live music ....

When we visit a beautiful place no matter how near or far, do we take time to take it in? Do we pause and appreciate the beauty around us?

Reflect:

May you fall asleep thinking about a beautiful place that you have visited.

Is there somewhere that you would like to go? Let your imagination free as you sleep tonight.

Star Gazing

We all have moments when we wonder where God is. Does He truly exist?
He seems so silent at times, so distant. We can say this is blasphemous as He
is always with us, but sometimes it doesn't feel like it.

At such times, going to the Bible can help, particularly Psalm 19 where God's
splendour is a tale that is written in the stars. Space itself tells His story
through the marvel of the heavens. His truth is on tour in the starry vault of
the sky, showing his skill in Creation's craftmanship.

I forget to look at the stars. I forget to walk outside and gaze at the beauty of
the night with the lights in the sky that God placed there. The Bible reminds
us that without a sound, we can see the glory of God. The stars are there
without fail every night, whether covered by cloud or not. We see God's
faithfulness and consistency as we notice the breath-taking night sky that
shows up evening upon evening.

Perhaps you are feeling that God has overlooked you. Perhaps you have been
waiting on a promise for years. Whatever the situation, could you look up at
the sky tonight and acknowledge His beauty and reassurance that He is
always there?

Reflect:

Could you step outside this week and look at the sky?

Storms Pass

As mentioned in another reflection, storms don't last forever. They can destroy homes and coastlines and even lives, but they subside, and the rhythm slowly returns to normal as people come together and rebuild and comfort one another.

Are you going through a storm in your life? Have you just come through one and are in the process of recovery? Can you see a storm brewing ahead? Rest in the knowledge that it will pass.

A storm reminds us how fragile we are. We cannot stand against the elements of nature during a cyclone. When we face storms in life, we sometimes have to relinquish control and wait for it to pass. Have you ever seen people trying to stand their ground during a storm? They must take shelter. They must move to a safer place.

Storms come in different forms. For example, a loved one with cancer, a traumatic event, a job loss, a divorce, death, a court case, and you can fill in the blank of a storm that has almost taken all your strength until you felt like you just couldn't anymore.

Hold on, don't let go. It will pass and life will slowly return.

Reflect:

Can you give yourself or someone you know time to heal, time to recover, time to take shelter? Can you adjust your expectations of yourself and others when facing a storm in life?

Walking

The philosopher Friedrich Nietzsche said that "it is only ideas gained from walking that have any worth." Perhaps this is a bit extreme for us to accept but he made his point.

When last did you wander, take a stroll, notice the goodness of God as you walked down your street?

Jesus walked a lot. Perhaps He de-stressed as He moved, perhaps He got fresh understanding and new ideas when He walked. He was fully human. Walking has been proven to improve creativity, physical wellness, mental health and it has other benefits.

When we walk, we don't abandon our thoughts, but we think differently. We see the same subject from different perspectives. We clear our minds and find inspiration again. We breathe deeply and we feel our feet on the ground as we move. Our blood circulates and we return energized and peaceful.

Walking is free and available to all. We don't need a lot of time either. A walk of 20 minutes will do the trick. No technology or calorie counting - it's not that type of walk. Just you and your God, children and partners and pets can come along sometimes.

Reflect:

Could you build a short walk into your weekly routine?

Slow Stream

Have you ever watched a stream flowing? Whether it's on a holiday or after a heavy rainfall, we can get lost in staring at the refreshing, clear water trickling and flowing down stream. The trick is not to get lost in watching one leaf or object that is floating. Before we know it, we get distracted by watching that one thing and we miss the peace of the gentle gaze of the flow.

Life can be like that sometimes. Gazing, appreciating something beautiful with family and friends whether it is something we are looking at or experiencing, we can become distracted by something so small that before we know it, we have allowed our thoughts to go down the river over something so small and we miss what is right in front of us.

Reflect:

Listen to the noises around you. Think about your special people sleeping in your home.

Can you decide to really be present?

Can you prevent the little distractions from taking you off course?

Sunshine

The rising sun is faithful and never changes. We know that it's there even when clouds obscure its view. It causes plants to grow, provides vitamin D, gives us a golden glow, and provides warmth on a winter's day. One of my favourite things to do is to lie on the grass in the sun with my dogs, and if I am lucky, one of my children too. Chatting and staring at the sky. When last did you cloud watch?

On a winter's day, when I am wrapped up and I go into the sun, I start to remove my layers as I get warmer. I don't always enjoy removing my layers of clothing. I have to bear my arms that feel exposed or hairy legs that need a wax. But it's good to feel that sunshine on my skin.

This got me thinking about another son, Jesus, the Son of God. He is as faithful as the rising sun; He brings us comfort and warmth and in His presence we seem to remove our layers of protection and self-preservation as He knows us deeply and loves us anyway.

When last did you hang out with the Son? Just chatting with silences in between, not in desperate prayer for an emergency but just chilling in His warm and beautiful presence, being with Him. We forget that sometimes Jesus wants to tell us things too and what He says is so beautiful.

Reflect:

Can you accept the relaxing peace, acceptance, and approval of Jesus?

Weather Patterns

Have you noticed that all of us, including family and friends, can exhibit certain "weather patterns"? We can imitate a storm, tornado, or thunderstorm depending on the day we have had.

When I find myself feeling like there is a black rain cloud following me around, I feel quite down. At other times I am like sunshine – bright, light, optimistic and open. My husband can walk through the door and be like a lightning storm after a tough day!

Just like the weather, these patterns in us subside after a while and sometimes we need to allow the storm to pass without trying to ignore the weather pattern or run from it. Allowing it to go through its process means eventually the sun will come out again.

Could we be graceful with each other? We can't dictate to others how they should behave. We can only control our response to them. The Bible tells us to "laugh with your happy friends when they're happy; share tears when they're down." (Romans12:15).

It's okay to not be calm and serene all the time. God gave us our emotions to experience and express. We just learn to do it in a way that doesn't hurt those around us. (And we don't always get that right either).

Reflect:

What was your "weather pattern" today? Why do you think this pattern was evident?

Blossom

When a plant blossoms, it grows and produces flowers. This is before the plant eventually bears fruit.

Sometimes we blossom where we least expect it. It is God who causes us to blossom and bloom. If we were responsible, then we could take credit for it. Do we actually see a plant blossom? Can we watch it? When the camera speeds up, we can watch the process on technology but with the naked eye, it is hard to watch the progress of flowers blossoming.

God sometimes places us in countries or places where we would rather not be. And in this place, He does something that only He can do. He grows and nurtures us and causes us to blossom and open and grow. Even when we don't feel it, He is working. Even when we don't see it, He is working.

Reflect:

Can you accept that God is working, causing you to bloom and blossom?

It may seem slow and invisible but trust His promises to come true.

Birds On a Branch

In 2020, the year of Covid lockdowns and restrictions, I had a dream where I saw birds sitting on a dry branch of a tree. Some dreams are just that – a dream that we have and forget about – and then there are other dreams that linger for weeks. This was the latter type of dream.

I knew that God was trying to show me something. I came across a quote a few weeks later – "A bird sitting on a tree is never afraid of the branch breaking because her trust is not on the branch but in its wings". It hit me in my chest. What was I afraid of? This was an opportunity in my life to fly, not to fail, not to run from but to embrace.

I feel like there is something to learn from this. When a "branch" in our lives breaks, whether it be in the form of losing a job or a broken relationship or perhaps financial stress or any situation where we feel like we are going to fall, remember that those are the times when we have the opportunity to fly. Even though we may flutter and not fly gracefully at first, we will find our thermal air current and our rhythm. Those things that were seemingly going to cause our fall will be our best opportunities to grow. We will use those talents that we didn't know we had.

Reflect:

Is there something in your life that has changed?

Could this be an invitation to be brave, to allow things to fall and for you to catch the wind of God's beautiful plan for your life and soar with Him?

Ocean Journey

At times we want life to be like a train ride as opposed to a sailboat. A train has a set track, you just decide on the destination. The track is set, and all the train has to do is get going. Life is more like a sailboat though – there are currents, winds, storms and no set track.

If we allow our children to believe that life is like a train ride, we set them up for disappointment. Let's encourage them to ride the wind, to persevere through the storms, to gather momentum with the currents and to enjoy the breeze when it's there.

Life isn't about arriving at a destination. It is each day, each beautiful moment with loved ones, friends, and co-workers. It's the challenges, victories, losses, hurts and celebrations. It's all beautiful but unpredictable and messy. Nature is so beautiful and there are no set lines in nature. Why would we be different? Life doesn't have to be perfect to be beautiful.

Reflect:

Whether it is a new idea, new job, school, or opportunity, could you cut the ropes from the moor and let your boat start to drift? God will be your rudder, guiding you and leading you.

Could you imagine yourself cutting the ropes and being courageous enough to set sail on the ocean of life?

Ride the Wave

The men in our family love to ride waves. Some waves are big and round, some small and closed out. There are so many different types and different conditions, and part of the fun I think is in the mystery of the ocean and the waves it creates.

We must ride waves in our lives. Perhaps you have ridden the wave of love in your life and found yourself gliding in the barrel of the wave, only to go over the falls and get hurt and nearly drown. Perhaps you are riding the work wave at the moment, feeling the bumpiness caused by the wind or the current and you have tried to make some moves on this wave or just keep your balance. Perhaps you have ridden the wave of partying and doing things your own way and you rode that wave too far and you don't know how to come back to paddle out again.

There are so many scenarios that could represent the waves we are riding and have ridden in our lives. Each wave requires effort; effort to paddle out, to wait, to know which wave to select and to know which wave or opportunity to let go.

The choice and commitment to paddle onto the wave and give it our best shot is ours. It's our decision to move with the force of the ocean underneath us, with the power and force of the water, to do what we can on it and keep standing.

Reflect:

What wave are you riding?

113

Temperature

I was in the shower the other day, adjusting the taps - a little hotter, no, a little more cold, ah, too much cold, until finally I reached that perfect temperature where I could put my head back and enjoy the water saturating my hair and body.

I felt like God spoke to me about my day, how I need to be adjusting the temperature all the time. Are there too many negative people around? Retreat a bit. Too much stress at work? Take a 5-minute walk and get a coffee and come back and breathe deeply. Too many financial burdens? Know that it is going to be okay and do things this weekend that don't cost money but are good for your soul. For example, going to the beach, for a hike, for a walk or a picnic and stare at the clouds.

We can't live our days in "hot water". We also can't live our days in "cold water". Reach out when you are feeling "cold", ask for help, go do some exercise.

Reflect:

Can you adjust the temperature until you are in that space where you know you can cope and be at peace, no matter where you are?

May your sleep be the perfect temperature of good dreams and peaceful rest.

Why do Birds Chirp in the Morning?

I asked my husband this question when we were walking through a small forest one Sunday afternoon. He said that the birds are discussing their plans for the day with their friends!

It seems that the morning is when male birds sing to attract mates and defend their territory. It takes a lot of energy to sing. The light is also dim for foraging and a perfect time to chirp. Unfortunately, due to artificial lighting and city noise, some birds have had their natural cycles disrupted. Changes in light can affect their body clock.

Have we, too, become affected by artificial elements that disrupt our natural rhythms and daily clocks? We find it difficult to sleep when we have been staring at our devices for hours. This is a form of artificial light and stimulation that has intruded into our lives.

Another thing that has changed the birds' lives is noise. Birds must change their chirping to be heard. In the city, it has been found that birds' songs are inclined to be faster and louder.

What does the noise do in our lives? Have we changed things in our lives due to the hustle and bustle, the "traffic" in our lives, the hooting and sounds of technology? Bombarded by social media telling us that we don't measure up becomes a noise in our heads.

Sometimes we can't hear the still whisper of God as we have too much noise around us.

I guess the question is: How can we turn the noise down and how can we keep our natural rhythms in sync in our modern world? The Bible says in Proverbs 1:20 that wisdom calls aloud in the open square and raises her voice n public. This verse shows that wisdom from God is available even in the noisy and busy market. Perhaps it is more about being aware of God being with us. His presence is everywhere we go, and we can draw on it whenever we need it. Asking God for wisdom in the noise, might mean that He leads you to a quiet bench in your lunch hour, or draws you to take some time in the evening to be still as opposed to being on autopilot and switching on the TV. It is the awareness that makes the difference.

Reflect:

Is your body in a natural cycle?

Do you go to bed at roughly the same time most nights?

Do you wake at roughly the same time most mornings?

Do you need to turn the "noise" down a little?

Running River

If we picture our life as a river, with its different meanders, bends, rapids, banks, and flows, we can allow our days to flow more easily. Perhaps we can avoid being caught up in panic when things don't go the way we plan.

We are all at different stages of the river.

When a relationship is new, and the water is in full flow with lots of energy and power, it seems that it will never dry up or run its course. At other times, we feel like the river is a trickle and we need a heavy downfall of rain to fill our river to help us get back into the momentum of the flow.

The banks of the river or the boundaries in our lives serve to protect us. With banks we can still move and get to where we are going, even if we are frustrated by them at times.

Once the river has run its course and enters the sea, it is open, vast, salty, and no longer a river.

Reflect:

Picture of a river. Which stage you are at?

What has run its course in your life? Can you let it be, let it flow and let go?

117

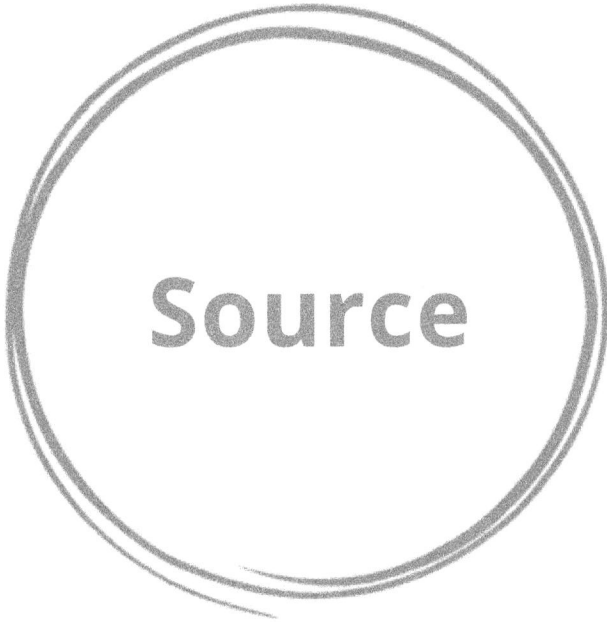

Source

Rest

The Bible tells us that God made the world in six days and on the seventh day He rested (Genesis 2:2). He is the creator of the Universe who has all power, who created the stars and the sea and the moon and the planets. And yet God rested.

If God rested, then I guess we should too. The Hebrew people were reprimanded by the prophets for not observing the Sabbath, i.e., for not resting. When we rest, we bring a completion to things as God did in creation.

Rest refreshes us and allows us to be more present. Rest gives us a fresh outlook on things. Society sometimes views rest as laziness or a lack of ambition, and yet it is the opposite. A clever person manages his time well enough to not compromise times of rest.

Reflect:

Could you commit to spend some time this week resting?

Just Three Questions

In February 2020, God encouraged me to ask Him three questions. It was as if Jesus was reclining on my bed with me, I could sense His peace and presence. I paused and gave it a lot of thought.

What would you ask God, if He gave you three questions?

I eventually decided on my three questions.

1- I asked Him if my entire family could know Him as a Father before they die.
2- I asked that my three children could be in one place with me and my husband in the following year or two (2 children live overseas)
3- I asked Him to refresh and strengthen my marriage.

I wept as I asked these questions as I realised what was important to me. It put things in perspective.

Reflect:

As you drift off, think about your three questions, and dare to ask them.

The Future

Some say if we visualise our future it will happen. I still don't own that house on the beach I have visualised for over 10 years now!

Others say we predict the future by creating it. We have choice and we have influence over all that we interact with, so we move forward and make the future we desire. But this doesn't predict illness or unexpected trials that come our way.

We know that God can see our future. He knows what it will be. He knows our choices too, even though He allows us to make them. Our brains are not developed enough to understand how this actually works. The Bible tells us that God knows the plans that He has for us and they are to prosper us and not to harm us (Jeremiah 29:11).

It also says that with our hearts we plan our lives, but the Lord establishes our steps (Proverbs 16:9). Perhaps this means that we should hold our plans lightly and be flexible with them. Perhaps we should plan but include God in our plan, asking Him for guidance and perspective and giving Him permission to change what needs to change. Then as we plan together with our Creator we co-create our future knowing that He is so good and never wants harm to come our way.

Reflect:

What do you want for your future? Can you picture it? Could you ask God for His input and perspective?

123

Anchor

When you think about an anchor, what picture comes to mind? The tattoo on an aging man's forearm? A rusty anchor at the entrance to a seafood restaurant? Something that is let down from a boat as we see it sinking in the murky water?

Whatever the images, there are a few truths about an anchor. An anchor is a symbol of safety where one can be still for a while and not drift off, a sense of stability. An anchor can be seen as a symbol of hope for the future for allowing us to grow where we are in the present as we look forward to the future.

We can also refer to a person as being our anchor – someone who supports us through our struggles, who is always there for us. God can be our anchor, keeping us from straying to where it is too dangerous, providing us with stability and security when we need it.

Reflect:

Do you accept that God is your anchor?

Is there an adventure you could plan, as long as you take your anchor with you?

Dreams

Do you ask God for dreams? He is so good and wants to give us good things. Sure, some dreams are pizza inspired, but some are from God. If you have a recurring dream, ask God to show you what it means.

God has been bringing people into my dreams that I haven't seen in a while. It is good to record our dreams. Whether it's speaking into your phone, or typing them out, it is worth the time. Asking God if the dream is from Him and waiting on the Holy Spirit to show us something is also an important step. I used to think that I needed to call the person I dreamt about and see how they were doing. This is not always the case.

One night I dreamt about someone, and I lifted them up in prayer and then planned to call them later that day. I then asked God to show me what the dream meant. It turned out to be about me, about how I had felt towards the person and that I needed to ask God to forgive me for that. There was no need to call at all.

We can also ask God for dreams when having to make a decision. God wants to talk to us and be involved in our decisions, He is a loving Father.

Reflect:

Have you ever had a recurring dream? What is it? Have you asked God what it means or have you shared it with someone you trust? Could you ask God to give you dreams?

Plug-In

Are we all connected to an "electricity" – a current that flows through all of us? I believe in the Spirit of God connecting us to one another. Perhaps you believe our human connection is through a different way.

We are all connected whether we like to admit it or not. Our current that we plug into is LOVE and it runs through all of us. We can choose to unplug ourselves and be alone but in doing so we lose the light that sustains us and trying to do things on your own, with no help from God is hard. I see God's love and presence as being that love and electricity that flows through us, connecting us all.

Reflect:

As you turn your light off to go to sleep tonight, remember to keep your inner light plugged into the source of all love.

Do you trust God to draw your power from Him?

Let God

How often do we want something so badly that we convince ourselves that it is what God wants too and no matter what, we are determined to make it happen? Chances are the desires of your heart are put there by God in the first place, but sometimes He protects us by delaying things until the time is right.

God is not a killjoy, He is good. Let Him open the doors, let His flow be your guide. Don't force things to happen, it is so exhausting. I tend to force and push and learn the hard way and then He graciously and quietly waits for me to trust Him and then all falls into place.

Reflect:

Is there something in your life that you are trying to force open?

Could you hand it over to God?

He's got you.

Jesus is the Vine

Many of us know the scripture in John chapter 15 that speaks about Jesus being the vine and we the branches and if we don't produce fruit, He will cut us off. Doesn't sound like the loving God that I know!

Whenever we read a scripture that goes against what we know to be God's character, it's good to dig a little deeper and find the original meaning.

We also need to investigate the context when we read scripture. When this scripture is used, it is talking about a vine. When a branch of the vine was not doing well, the vine dresser would pick it up and support it by placing it on a trellis type of apparatus so that it would grow. The word "cut off" in verse 2 actually comes from the Greek phrase which can also be translated "he takes up [to himself] every fruitless branch." He doesn't remove these branches, but He takes them to Himself. As the wise and loving farmer, He lifts them up off the ground to enhance their growth.

This is the God I know who never gives up on us. He helps us but never discards us. Know that no matter what you have ever done, He will never cut you off or abandon you.

Reflect:

Keep looking for the truth in a situation that you are finding challenging, the real truth.

Access

It's embarrassing to admit, but I used to believe that going to a therapist and even a doctor (eek!) wasn't necessary if you had enough faith. What a pressure to live under. Thankfully, I don't believe that anymore. God is so much more accessible than that. He is not distant in the sky only sending down healing and restoration in certain conditions. He can be found in the support of a psychologist, He can be found in the wisdom of a doctor, in the conversation and care of a friend, in the smile of the supermarket cashier, in the voice of a stranger.

God is so accessible to us. He doesn't want it to be hard for us to engage with Him and He chose to live and dwell within us and if He can use a donkey to talk in the Bible, then He can use anyone to show us His will, His love, His acceptance, His approval, His grace. The Bible says that we have permanent access to God's kindness (Psalm 145:9).

So why do we think that we are exempt from feeling really down when the trials of life become too much to bear? Why do we sometimes think that as Christians we should believe for healing when God could be providing our healing through medicine? God is God and can work any way that He chooses to. It is not for us to limit Him to our version of who He is in our heads. He is way bigger than that.

Reflect:

Would you allow God to use people you encounter to show you aspects of who He is and what He is saying to you? Could you notice people tomorrow and be aware of His loving kindness in those you encounter?

Faith

I felt like God showed me that when things are easy in life and all is flowing, it seems easy to believe and have faith. How do we exercise our faith muscles unless we need to lean on God for things? When something turns out different to how we planned or how we expected, can we take it to God?

Ask for His help. He promises to give it to us. He always has a plan and it is never to trip us up. It is always for our good.

Life is messy, unpredictable and tough sometimes. If it weren't hard sometimes, how would we celebrate the good times? To know the valley, we need to climb the mountain. To know a high, we have to experience a low. These sayings ring true to what we know. Life is beautiful and life is heart breaking. Through it all, God is at our side. Allow Him in.

Reflect:

Could you courageously trust your Heavenly Father for something you are battling with?

Sleep peacefully tonight knowing that He is in control.

Wait

One of my children surfed competitively. One of our favourite destinations where the national surfing championships took place is Jefferey's Bay, South Africa. It is famous for the world renown surf break called Supertubes.

On our first trip there, I took a picture of a place that was quaint with a wooden balcony that overlooked Pepper Street that looks onto Supertubes. I had a secret desire in my heart to stay there one day but I didn't tell anyone. Only God knew about it. I fantasized about what it would be like to stay there, carefree and on the beach with the best coffee and croissant bistro downstairs. And so I went on being a mother of three children and working and doing life.

10 years later, my husband and I went on a road trip that included stopping in Jefferey's Bay overnight. My husband booked the accommodation, and when we arrived…. I took a picture again, the same one! He had booked the exact room and place that I had dreamed about 10 years previously.

God hears it all. He hears our deepest inmost desires; He hears every prayer and every longing. He doesn't operate on our time schedule. He is so so so so good.

Reflect:

Can you give God time?

Papa

In South Africa we have a beautiful mountain range called the Drakensburg. Visiting any part of this area is food for the soul. I remember going there on a trip with my husband and one morning I woke up with the words, "Morning Papa" rolling off my tongue. Tears started to roll down my cheeks. If I didn't hear God say anything to me. These two words literally took my breath away. It's like He had a new name for me to call Him: Papa. So intimate, so close, so strong, so reassuring.

God is our Papa, He adores us. He wants what is best for us and He jealously watches over us and protects us. He is so close and wants us to lean against His chest and hear what He is saying. He will never say anything to belittle us, to make us feel guilty or embarrass us. That is not what a loving Papa does.

Reflect:

Could you ask your Papa in heaven for something tonight?

Do you believe that He wants to bless you?

Fairy Tale

We all grew up watching fairy tales with "happily ever after". Nowadays I love that children's movies involve different characters than when I was growing up. For example, the cartoon Mohana involves a heroine who saves her village (as opposed to being rescued by a handsome prince).

Yet there remains an overriding sense that life's goal is bliss and peace and happily ever after.

Admitting that life isn't a fairy tale isn't being negative or pessimistic. It is merely admitting that life is full of challenges and sometimes chaos and that in the midst of it, we have a God who doesn't leave us to fend for ourselves or solve our own problems. He draws alongside us and helps us and comforts us and gives us wisdom.

The Holy Spirit invites us to come alive in the chaos, not to remove us from it. Once our perspective on life shifts and we see the realistic picture, it sets us free to embrace the difficult and the not so perfect experiences we find ourselves having.

Reflect:

Can you ask God to show you that He is always with you?

Illuminate What's Right in Front of Me

We all have regrets and wonder what life would have been like, had we chosen a different path. Our life has twists and turns and we cannot go back and relive a different choice. Some of us spend time wanting a life different from what we have, yet we cannot go back.

What we tend to forget is that the future is full of possibilities and choices that we can make. We have learnt lessons from the past that affects what we choose today and the paths we didn't take have influenced who we are today.

We don't know how life would have turned out if we hadn't given up that sport we loved, or if we had stayed married or if we had travelled to India when we had the opportunity. I suspect it wouldn't have worked out the way we romanticise it in our heads.

Could we dare to believe that the life we are living is where God meets us? Can we believe that He is good and loving and works all things for good. Even our mistakes? Can He use those for good?

Reflect:

Do you regret any decisions you have made in life?

Could you bring them to mind and then release them to God, like letting balloons go in a field. Watch them float away and trust God with your life as it is now.

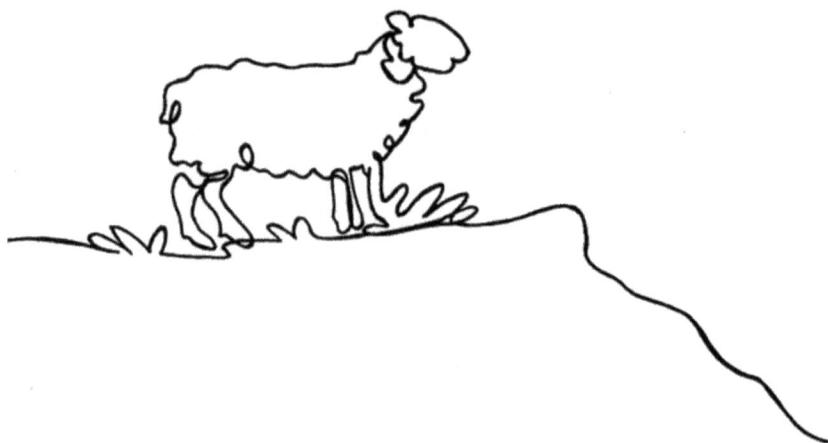

Good Shepherd

God, my shepherd!
I don't need a thing.
You have bedded me down in lush meadows,
you find me quiet pools to drink from.
True to your word,
you let me catch my breath
and send me in the right direction.
Even when the way goes through
Death Valley,
I'm not afraid
when you walk at my side.
Your trusty shepherd's crook
makes me feel secure.
You serve me a six-course dinner
right in front of my enemies.
You revive my drooping head;
my cup brims with blessing.
Your beauty and love chase after me
every day of my life.
I'm back home in the house of God
for the rest of my life.

Psalm 23 is medicine for a peaceful sleep! Read it through again,
pausing where you need to.

References

For More Information about the author
contact her by email:

deana.steyn@gmail.com

www.ingramcontent.com/pod-product-compliance
Lightning Source LLC
Chambersburg PA
CBHW052011090426
42741CB00008B/1651